T0402755

PANGOLINS AT RISK

SAVING THESE ARMORED ANIMALS

BY KATHRYN CLAY

CAPSTONE PRESS
a capstone imprint

Published by Capstone Press, an imprint of Capstone
1710 Roe Crest Drive, North Mankato, Minnesota 56003
capstonepub.com

Library of Congress Cataloging-in-Publication Data is available on the Library
of Congress website.

ISBN: 9798875222030 (hardcover)
ISBN: 9798875221989 (paperback)
ISBN: 9798875221996 (ebook PDF)

Summary: Pangolins may be covered in armor, but they are at risk of extinction.
Readers will learn what is putting these armored animals in danger, including
hunting, severe weather, and habitat loss, as well as what people are doing to
help them.

Editorial Credits
Editor: Ashley Kuehl; Designer: Elijah Blue; Media Researcher: Jo Miller;
Production Specialist: Tori Abraham

Image Credits
Alamy: Phil Judd Photography, 19, Scott Hurd, 11 (top), Vuk Valcic, 21, 27;
Getty Images: Catherine Delahaye, 29, Fabian von Poser, 23, imageBROKER/
Fabian von Poser, 13, iStock/Asim Patel, cover, iStock/Vicky_Chauhan, 12;
Newscom: Rhino Revolution/Magnus/SIPA, 8; Shutterstock: Binturong-
tonoscarpe, 6, DeawSS, 4 (heart icon), Eric Isselee, 15, Holly Auchincloss,
14, imranhridoy, 4 (trees icon), Jishith Jayaram, 25, nexusby, 4 (temperature
icon), Stefan Balaz, 4 (arrow icon), Steven Dudka, 9, Vector Designer Tanvir,
throughout (pangolin icon), Vickey Chauhan, 7, Viktor Tanasiichuk, 11 (map);
Superstock: Gilles Nicolet/Biosphoto, 5, Suzi Eszterhas/Minden Pictures, 17, 28

Design Elements:
Shutterstock: Pixels Park, Textures and backgrounds

Printed and bound in China. 006276

TABLE OF CONTENTS

Words in **bold** are in the glossary.

WHAT MAKES AN ANIMAL ENDANGERED?

NUMBER OF ANIMALS:
VERY LOW OR SHRINKING FAST

HABITAT LOSS:
BIG DECREASE IN NATURAL HABITAT

RANGE REDUCTION:
SHRINKING AREA WHERE IT CAN LIVE

BREEDING DECLINE:
FEWER ANIMALS HAVING YOUNG

THREATS:
HIGH RISK OF POACHING,
DISEASE, OR CLIMATE CHANGE

CHAPTER 1
A DAY IN THE LIFE

Evening falls in a tropical forest. A pangolin stirs. It begins its search for food. The pangolin roams the night alone. Its sharp sense of smell finds ants and termites. The pangolin's long, sticky tongue licks up the insects.

The pangolin is full. It finds a safe place to rest. A hollow tree gives protection from **predators**. Soon daylight approaches. The pangolin curls its body in a tight ball for sleep.

A tree pangolin in Cameroon

Pangolins are **nocturnal** mammals found in Africa and Asia. They have an unusual appearance. Their bodies are covered in tough scales. They have long tongues. These features have earned them the nickname "scaly anteater."

Pangolins are private animals. They live alone. They use scent to mark their homes and keep others away. They live and move quietly. Hiding spots include hollow trees or burrows. Their behaviors make it difficult to study them.

A Sunda pangolin is also known as a Javan or a Malayan pangolin.

An Indian pangolin curls up to protect itself.

PANGOLIN TRIVIA

QUESTION: What other mammals are covered in scales?

ANSWER: None! Pangolins are the only mammals with scales covering their whole body.

AT RISK

Scientists can only estimate the pangolin population. They know the **species** cannot survive the large number hunted each year. **Poachers** are a major threat. They target the animals for their meat and scales. The illegal hunters have ways to track and capture the animals.

Many people pay high prices for pangolin meat and scales. They think the meat is fancy. They believe the scales can treat illness. The high demand and cost mean more pangolins are hunted.

Scales from pangolins poached in South Africa

This pangolin was captured and taken to a market to be sold.

PANGOLIN TRIVIA

QUESTION: Can pangolin scales treat illness?

ANSWER: No! This belief is incorrect. There is no proof that pangolin scales have any medical benefit.

CHAPTER 2
GET TO KNOW PANGOLINS

Eight different pangolin species have been identified. Four are in Africa. The other four live in Asia. Each species has unique habitats, physical features, and behaviors.

African pangolins have a variety of habitats. They live in savannas, forests, and grasslands. Asian pangolins are often found in tropical forests.

Pangolins use their claws to dig deep burrows for sleeping. Some sleep in hollow trees or logs.

WHERE PANGOLINS LIVE

ARCTIC OCEAN

NORTH AMERICA

EUROPE

ASIA

ATLANTIC OCEAN

AFRICA

PACIFIC OCEAN

PACIFIC OCEAN

INDIAN OCEAN

SOUTH AMERICA

RANGE

N
W E
S

AUSTRALIA

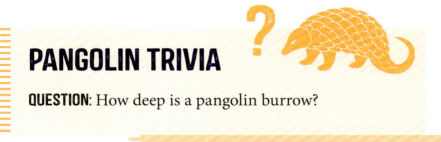

PANGOLIN TRIVIA

QUESTION: How deep is a pangolin burrow?

ANSWER: Some burrows are large enough for a human to stand up in.

PHYSICAL FEATURES

Pangolins look unique. Their bodies are covered in thick, overlapping scales. The scales are made of keratin. They grow throughout a pangolin's life. If pangolins lose a scale, a new one can grow. Asian pangolins have hair growing between their scales. African pangolins do not.

The Indian pangolin does not climb trees.

The ground pangolin, or Temminck's pangolin, lives in southern Africa.

Pangolin species are different sizes. The smallest is the long-tailed pangolin. It weighs about 3.5 pounds (1.6 kilograms). The giant pangolin can weigh more than 70 pounds (32 kg). It can grow up to 5 feet (1.5 meters) long.

PANGOLIN TRIVIA

QUESTION: What else is made of keratin?

ANSWER: Human nails and hair are made of keratin. So are rhino horns.

WEAPONS AND DEFENSES

Lions, tigers, hyenas, and wild dogs hunt pangolins. A pangolin's scales are its main defense. When a predator is near, the pangolin curls into a tight ball. The scales are hard to bite or claw through.

Pangolins hiss and whip their tails to warn predators. They also release a strong smell. The smell marks their territory. It keeps other pangolins away. None of these defenses keep them safe from their biggest predator—poachers.

A pangolin rolls into a ball to stay safe from lion cubs.

MATCHING GAME

Make 24 Cards: On eight of them, write the name of a pangolin species. On the next four, write "Africa." Write "Asia" on four more. Finally, write a unique feature of each species on each of the last eight cards.

Goal: Mix up the cards. Then try to match each species card with its habitat and unique feature cards.

PANGOLIN	HABITAT	UNIQUE FEATURE
Chinese	Asia	larger scales relative to its body size
Indian	Asia	thick, broad tail
Sunda	Asia	spends a lot of time in trees
Philippine	Asia	body is slender and smaller than other pangolins
Temminck's	Africa	spends most of its time on the ground
Giant	Africa	largest of all pangolin species
Tree	Africa	tail that can grip branches as it climbs
Black-Bellied	Africa	tail is longer than its body

LIFE CYCLE

A pangolin's life cycle starts with the birth of a single pup. Babies are born with soft white scales. The scales harden after a few days. Pups are defenseless until then. Young pangolins ride on their mother's tail for safety. If predators are near, mothers protect the pups. The mother may roll into a ball. Her pup is tucked safely inside.

Around age two, babies leave their mothers. They live alone until it's time to find a mate. After that, much of their life cycle is a mystery. No one knows how long most pangolins live in the wild. Few survive long in captivity.

A two-week-old Chinese pangolin on its mother's tail

PANGOLIN TRIVIA

QUESTION: What is a baby pangolin called?

ANSWER: A pangopup.

FOOD AND FOOD SOURCES

Pangolins play an important role in their environments. They help to control the ant and termite populations. One pangolin can eat up to 70 million insects each year. Sometimes they can't find ants or termites. Then they may eat flies, worms, and crickets.

A strong sense of smell helps pangolins find food. First, they sniff out an ant nest. Then their strong front claws dig up the nest. Pangolin tongues reach deep into the ground. Special muscles keep their noses and ears closed. Insects can't get in. The ants stick to the tongue and are swallowed whole.

Insects stick to the pangolin's long, thin tongue.

— CHAPTER 3 —
ENDANGERED STATUS

The **endangered** status of pangolins depends on the species. Some African pangolins are considered vulnerable. They could become endangered. Others are already endangered. All Asian pangolins are endangered or critically endangered. Very few of them are left. Without help, pangolins could become **extinct**.

Conservation groups help pangolins. Their work includes anti-poaching laws and habitat restoration. Scientists also teach local communities about the animals' importance.

A pangolin at an animal sanctuary in Zimbabwe

PANGOLINS IN CAPTIVITY

Some endangered animals live safely in **sanctuaries**. Guards keep poachers away. But pangolins don't do well there. They become stressed and sick. They also have particular tastes. They only eat insects from their home areas. Pangolins in captivity often refuse to eat and starve to death.

HUMAN-MADE RISKS

Pangolins are sold more than any other animal. Nearly one in five animals sold illegally is a pangolin. Much of the poaching happens in Asia.

Pangolins don't run or fight. They are easy to catch. Poachers only need to find them and pick them up. Weapons and traps aren't needed.

In Africa, pangolins used to be sold only for meat. But that is changing. The Asian pangolin population is decreasing. But people in Asia still want pangolin scales. So poachers catch African species instead. They sell the scales in Asia.

PANGOLIN TRIVIA

QUESTION: How many pangolins have been killed since 2010?

ANSWER: From 2010 to 2019, more than 1 million pangolins were killed.

A man holds a long-tailed pangolin in Cameroon.

ENVIRONMENTAL RISKS

Poachers pose the biggest threat to pangolins. But pangolins also face environmental dangers. Forests are cut down to make way for farming and roads. Pangolins lose their habitats. Climate change means more forest fires and floods. These events destroy animals' homes and affect their food sources.

Changes in environment can cause stress for an animal. Stress weakens a pangolin's ability to fight off diseases. Contact with humans can also bring viruses.

Natural predators are a threat too. These include leopards, lions, hyenas, and large birds. Scales offer some protection. But pangolins cannot always escape.

A forest in India is cut down for farming.

CHAPTER 4

HOW TO HELP

People around the world are working to save pangolins. Countries have agreed to **international** laws. These laws make it illegal to buy or sell pangolins. People caught selling pangolins in China, Vietnam, and India can face big fines or jail.

Conservation groups rescue captured pangolins. They return them to forests. These groups also teach about the importance of protecting pangolins.

PANGOLIN TRIVIA

QUESTION: When is World Pangolin Day?

ANSWER: The third Saturday in February.

A ground pangolin at a sanctuary in Zimbabwe

GROUPS WORKING TO HELP PANGOLINS

PANGOLIN CRISIS FUND:

Raises money to stop the demand for pangolin products.

RAINFOREST ACTION NETWORK:

Works to preserve rainforests, protect the climate, and uphold human rights.

SAVE PANGOLINS:

Supports conservation in Asia and Africa. Raises awareness around the world.

An educator at a program in Vietnam teaches a boy about pangolins.

Every action adds up. Students can help by spreading the word. Many people don't even know what pangolins are. Sharing this information is a big step. Teaching people about pangolins will encourage them to help.

Another way to help is to shop responsibly. Talk to the people in your family who do the shopping. Ask them not to buy products made in rainforests or other protected areas. Support companies that protect the environment. These companies might work to reduce waste or use recycled materials.

LETTER TO LAWMAKERS

In 2023, then-President Joe Biden wrote a letter to Congress. He wanted to stop the illegal trade of pangolin products. He pushed for stricter laws and worldwide cooperation to stop poachers.

Write a letter to lawmakers in your city or state. Ask them to support programs that protect pangolins. Include facts about why pangolins are important. Describe why their population is in danger. Explain why we need stronger laws to protect them. Ask an adult to help you find contact information and share your letter.

GLOSSARY

conservation (khan-sur-VAY-shun)—wise use and protection of natural resources

endangered (en-DANE-jurd)—at risk of dying out

extinct (ik-STINGKT)—no longer living; an extinct animal has died out.

international (in-tur-NASH-uh-nuhl)—having to do with more than one country

nocturnal (nahk-TUR-nuhl)—active at night

poach (POHCH)—to illegally hunt an animal; people who poach are called poachers.

predator (PRED-uh-tur)—an animal that hunts other animals for food

sanctuary (SANGK-choo-er-ee)—a place where animals are cared for and protected

species (SPEE-sheez)—a group of animals that share common traits

READ MORE

Eszterhas, Suzi. *Operation Pangolin: Saving the World's Only Scaled Mammal*. Minneapolis: Millbrook Press, 2023.

Reddy, Christopher. *A Kids Book about Being a Scientist*. New York: DK Children, 2025.

Rocco, Hayley, and John Rocco. *Hello, I'm a Pangolin*. New York: G.P. Putnam's Sons, 2024.

INTERNET SITES

Rainforest Action Network: Pangolin
ran.org/wildlife-factsheet/pangolin/

National Geographic Kids: Pangolin
kids.nationalgeographic.com/animals/mammals/facts/pangolin

World Wildlife Fund: Pangolin
worldwildlife.org/species/pangolin

INDEX

ABOUT THE AUTHOR

Kathryn Clay has written more than 100 nonfiction books for kids. Her books cover a wide range of topics, including everything from sign language to space travel. When she's not writing, Kathryn works at a college, helping students develop their critical thinking and study skills. She holds master's degrees in literature and creative writing from Minnesota State University, Mankato.

Kathryn lives in southern Minnesota with her family and an energetic goldendoodle. Together, they make sustainable, eco-friendly choices whenever possible.